The Ultimate Success Formula

(Newly updated! 2.0)

"Mastery Made Simple

~ With the 3 Pillars of Success"

By

Marcus Geier

(the Metaphysical Philanthropist)

Published in 2019 by 13 StarGates Publishing
A Division of MoonCoach™ LLC.
www.13StarGates.com

Always Start with the End in Mind

Target market: People who want to gain Mastery of their life and learn exactly how to achieve their goals, how long it will take, and know with certainty why some goals are not being achieved, and how to correct that.

Thesis: There is a simple, proven formula for Success that can be used as a yardstick, benchmark, and blueprint for achieving any desired goal.

Success:

> *"Success is making continual progress toward YOUR goals."*
>
> *~ Marcus Geier*

"No problem can be solved from the same level of consciousness that created it." *- Albert Einstein*

The Problem: You have not achieved one of your desired goals.
Level of consciousness of the problem: The material level or (3D).
Level of consciousness of the solution: The mental level (5D).
Tracking Indicator: Your emotional state.
Solution Process: The Ultimate Success Formula.

TABLE OF CONTENTS

Introduction: GOOD NEWS!

Success, achievement, wealth, health and love are far easier to understand and get than you imagined! They are your natural state. This brilliant book will quickly equip you with the secret knowledge and simple tools to begin achieving your goals and dreams quickly and consistently.

This book answers your questions such as:

> Is there a science to success?
> Is there a mathematical formula for success?
> Why do others have success but I struggle so hard for so little?
> **How can I consistently get what I want?**
> How does life work anyway?
> How can I know whether a goal is right for me?
> How can I tell whether or not a goal is achievable for me?
> Why do I achieve some goals and not others?
> Is there a goal benchmark I can use?
> And many more…

For most people, success seems elusive, difficult, inconsistent and just plain hard. It's not. You simply need the formula. Success becomes simple when you **USE** the formula!

If you choose to truly learn the formula and actually use the tool daily, you WILL know how to get everything you want! You will know exactly why some of your goals have been achieved and others not, and what to do about that.

While the formula may seem basic and simple, the magic is in the nuance. Giving you the formula is simply not enough. The context for each part is vital. I've done that for you in this book.

Please read carefully, thoughtfully and integrate the small details - they make a huge difference! Then read the book again and again until you've reached unconscious competence in these principles. Then your life will become ever more easy, graceful and fulfilling! Does that sound fun?

Let's make magic in YOUR life NOW!

Your friend and guide,
Marcus Geier

Element 1 Clarity

Clarity: How can you get what you want until you know what you want? This seems basic and simple. But is it? 99% of people worldwide fail because they don't know exactly what they want. While many of them think they do, they actually don't, often because their stated "want" is not authentic to THEM. We'll get to that soon.

Business success is predicated on strategic thinking. Strategic thinking and strategic planning are the most important functions of not only a business owner, but everyone seeking success in any area of their life. The same is true for attaining blissful relationships, vibrant health, secure and sustainable affluence, happiness and satisfaction.

What is strategic thinking? Strategic is asking the "what" and the "why" questions. The "what" question is: "What do I really, really, really, want?" This is the single most important question in the world. This question needs to be asked all the time under all circumstances everywhere, every day. When you start adopting this question as your primary question throughout your day, you will see a massive positive sea-change shift in your life.

(Do you remember when you started using a GPS? That changed everything about traveling, right? Using a GPS requires that you input a destination - a clear and specific destination, otherwise it merely shows you where you are.) Adopting this primary question will change everything about your life.

> *When you notice yourself arguing with your spouse, child or co-worker, stop and ask yourself: "What do I really want from this?" "Do I really want to convince them I'm right or do I really want to have a loving, harmonious relationship?" That will shift your behaviour and defuse the argument. [The need to be right comes directly from your ego-self that was formed as a young child. You do not want to let your ego run the show.]*
>
> *When you are deciding on what to eat, stop and ask yourself: "What do I really want from this food?" "Do I really want to appease my taste buds to get a short-term sugar-rush or do I really want to create vibrant sustainable health?"*
>
> *When you are deciding on where to spend your money, stop and ask yourself: "What do I really want from this money?" "Do I really need that new iphone to get a short-term buying-rush or do I really want to invest in my future financial security?"*

The "WHY" question is: "why do I want that?" This is almost as important as "what" do you want because the "why" question clarifies the authenticity of what you want. So every time you state what you want, follow it up with: "Why do I want that?" When you answer that, then ask: "Why do I want that?" And keep on asking until you get to a root cause "why". This is incredibly important as I will highlight with the following story.

> *So my friend Bob said to me, "Marcus, I want a brand new red Ferrari convertible!"*
> *I replied, "That's great Bob, why do you want that?"*

Well that question certainly took him aback.
"Why, he asked? Well, so when I drive around town I'll feel like a million bucks."
"Great Bob", I replied, "Why do you want that?"

Again he was taken aback and thought a moment and said: "Well, when I drive around town in my new Ferrari, I'll see people looking at me and I'll feel really good about myself."
To which I responded: "Great Bob why do you want that?"

He looked at me slightly annoyed and replied: "Well when I see them looking at me they'll be thinking, wow he's really successful."
"Why do you want that Bob?"

"When I see them looking at me I'll FEEL successful."
"Okay Bob, why do you want that?"

"Well, I guess I have low self-esteem", as he dejectedly looked at the floor.
"Okay Bob I think we got down to the root cause 'why'. So Bob, will buying a new Ferrari solve your self-esteem problem?"

He thought for a while, cocked his head to the side, and then replied: "Well, maybe for a week or two, but after that I guess reality will set back in."

"Correct!" I exclaimed. "So if what you really really really want is to feel really good about yourself, feel successful, and feel satisfied with your life, and you realize that getting a new Ferrari convertible will not do that permanently or long-term, what do you think you should be doing?"

He responded, "Well, I guess I need to find some ways to

permanently fix my self-esteem problems by coaching with you."

"Bob, that's going to be a whole lot easier and cheaper and longer-lasting than buying a Ferrari, isn't it?"

"Yes!", he replied.

So what have we learned from this little story? The fact of the matter is that most people most of the time say they want things when in fact those things will not directly give them what they are really seeking. They are not authentic wants. Those things are what they think will give them what they really want (a means to an end), which always comes down to feeling a certain way.

Let's emphasize this vital point. Always determine whether your goal is an end goal or simply a means to an end. A means-to-an-end goal is not authentic and we'll explore why that will kill your goal-achievement in a later chapter.

Your chosen goals MUST be 100% authentic for YOU.

Another example is: I could ask Suzy what she wants. And she'll say:

"I want a beautiful house with 5 bedrooms on a huge lot in a good part of town with a big back yard all fenced in. I want this house to be a comfortable, spacious safe space. I want a huge family room that's attached to a big kitchen."

Then I ask her why she wants that, and she replies:

"Well because I just got married and we want to have 4 children and we want a spacious safe house in a great school district to raise our family and to have big family dinners with our parents and siblings and I want a big yard where the kids can play with the dogs and I can keep an eye on them and provide them a really good quality of life."

Now I can ask Debbie what she wants.

And Debbie says she wants a big 5 bedroom house on a huge lot in a good part of town with a big fenced yard. When I ask Debbie why, she replies with:

"Well everybody told me when I was growing up I wouldn't amount to anything and we lived in a crappy little house in the poor part of town and I want to show everybody that I'm a big success and they were wrong about me."

We can see that Susie's "WHY" for her big house is very authentic. The house is the end goal. The house will give her what she really wants. So that is a goal that she can achieve because it is authentically congruent with all parts of her.

Debbie, on the other hand, wants the house for reasons that are not directly tied to the house. She thinks that the house (a means to an end) will give her what she really wants (to feel successful and recognized for it). She hasn't stopped to consider what it is that she really wants. If she does she will realize the house is not necessarily an effective avenue to achieve what she wants.

Her life would be better served by figuring out exactly what she wants and going directly after that without wasting huge time and resources taking interim steps. Chasing an incongruent goal will result in one of two outcomes: 1) It won't be achieved. 2) It can sometimes be achieved with enough drive but will not be satisfying.

Now here is a key point. The 1st most important defining characteristic of all successful people is:

Clarity of Vision.

Really.

The 1st defining characteristic of super-successful people is: Clarity of Vision.

> Successful people know exactly what they want.
> Successful people choose goals that are authentic for them.
> Successful people focus on exactly what they want.
> Successful people continually talk about exactly what they want.

Unsuccessful people do NOT know exactly what they want, they focus on what they don't want, they talk about what they don't want, and they continually make excuses, blame other people or circumstances and do not take personal responsibility.

> Which one have you mostly been until now?
> Which one do you now choose to be?

Imagine walking into a gigantic restaurant with a massive menu that has every sort of wonderful food available. You are seated at a terrific table. A waiter comes over with his pad and pencil and asks you what he can get you for dinner.

You look at the menu and say: *"Well, I don't really feel like pasta"*. The waiter asked what he can get you for dinner. You say *"Well, I don't really feel like beef"*. The waiter asked what he can get you for dinner. You reply with *"Well, I don't really feel like fish"*. How long can this go on before the waiter walks away in frustration?

Now imagine walking into that same restaurant. You sit down, the waiter comes over and you say: *"This is what I'd like to drink, I would like this for an appetizer, for my main course I would like this and this and this with this on the side cooked this way, and for dessert I'll have that with a coffee made this way"*. The waiter smiles, writes it all down, and says: *"Thank you, I'll be right back with your meal!"*

Which scenario do you choose day by day?

On the first page of this book, I defined success as:

Success is making continual progress toward your goals.

The assumption here is that you DO KNOW what your goals are. The bottom line is this.

***You cannot get what you want until
you know exactly what you want.***

What happens when you don't know what you want? Nothing? It's way worse...

***If you don't know what you want,
you will get what other people want for you.***

You are surrounded by people, companies, advertisers and governments that want all kinds of things from you and for you. If you don't say what you do want with great clarity and focus, you will get what THEY want for you. Is that how you want to live your life? Well guess what. That's how 99% of the planet lives their life most of the time in most areas. Do you want to be the 99% or the 1%? Do you want to know what the 1% do that you're not doing yet?

Numerous large-scale studies have shown that 1% of the world's population are successful according to their own definitions, and 99% are not. Those 1% have more wealth than the 99% combined! Numerous large-scale studies have shown that 1% of the world has clear written down goals for every major area of their life. 99% do not. Well guess what? That 1% are the same. There is a 100% cause and effect relationship between having clear written down goals for every area of your life and being successful. It really is that simple and basic.

Now here's the thing: most people on this planet have heard about the importance of goal setting. You probably heard it all your life, from your parents, your teachers, your professors and every book, CD or seminar on personal growth that you have been exposed to. They all start with setting goals.

I've actually tested this out with thousands of my college students over many years. I taught working adults for over 13 years, and I taught over 5,000 of them how to set goals, why to set goals, gave them a goal setting spreadsheet and actually made them do it by assigning a grade to it. (Some still didn't do it!)

I met many of them in subsequent years in the hallways. They always immediately recognized me and said: *"Hi Professor Marcus, how are you doing? Good to see you!"* To which I always responded: *"It's great to see you. How is your life going?"*

I always received one of 2 basic answers. Either they responded with: *"Oh I'm just hanging in there."*(99%) Or, *"I'm doing great!"*(1%).

My next question always was: *"Do you remember me teaching you the goal setting process and are you keeping up with your spreadsheet?"* 100% of the time there was a direct correlation between their life going great and their keeping up with the goals!

100% of the time there was a direct correlation between them just hanging in there and them having forgotten to keep up with their goals.

What I heard frequently from those that were keeping up with their goals was something like: *"Wow, now that I think about it, 75% of those goals have been achieved in the past year. It's amazing! I don't know how that happened, it's kind of magical."* To which I smiled.

So my question to you right now is this. Are you going to be one of the 1% or are you going to be one of the 99%? If you choose to be one of the 1% then you know exactly what you must do. If you don't do this right now, then ask yourself why and figure out why. It means that you are hanging on to some deep and very serious self-sabotaging, limiting unconscious beliefs. Get rid of them now!

(Note: Unconscious beliefs are nothing more than thought-habits glued with the emotion of a traumatic experience - usually prior to age 7. By becoming aware of them, they are no longer SUBconscious. At the conscious level, you can quickly replace them and then just monitor your thought-habits until you've installed a new, more functional thought-habit.)

Stop right here, right now and write out at least one major goal, by hand, on paper. Sticky notes are perfect. Sign it, date it and tape it to your bathroom mirror. That is a vital first step. Start it with: *"I will apply all of my power to achieve the following aim: _____."* Then write your goal, in present tense, as if already achieved using all senses if possible. Everytime you see it, declare it out loud with enthusiasm. If that doesn't put a huge smile on your face and invigorate you, then you need a goal that you passionately desire because this one is not congruent with YOU.

How to hang with successful people:

It is super-important to realize that successful people do business with other successful people. They do NOT do business with unsuccessful people. Why? Successful people will tend to continue being successful because they think differently than unsuccessful people. How do they know? There are clear markers.

You've likely been out to lunch or dinner with successful and unsuccessful people. Successful people take about 15 seconds to order. Unsuccessful people take several minutes and often require the server to come back once or more.

How we do anything tends to be how we do everything.

That is one way that successful people know who they want to do business with.

Successful people

- Know exactly what they want, whether for lunch, a spouse, a business project or health.
- Are decisive and make decisions very quickly.
- Are always focused on what they want and therefore only talk about what they want.
- Take responsibility for their lives.
- Are ruthless about who they spend time with.
- Do not watch TV, especially "news".
- Do not whine, complain, blame, shame, make excuses or justify.
- See failure as simply an unexpected outcome and an opportunity to make a new decision.

- Don't take things personally.
- Think strategically and hold the long-term view.
- Tend to be happy, even when grouchy - some get a positive emotional payoff from being grouchy.
- Are optimistic - always.
- Do not suffer fools and they will not be in the presence of negative people.
- Are disciplined about their personal habits.
- Love to have fun.
- Live in a safe Universe.
- Absolutely KNOW that things will work out no matter how things look now.

In order to be accepted by successful people, you'll need to adopt these characteristics. Better yet, as you work to adopt and integrate these characteristics, you will absolutely become ever more successful!

Successful people:
1. Are highly intuitive.
2. Immediately write down their intuitive hits.
3. Always act on them as soon as possible.

So what can we conclude now. The first element of the ultimate success formula is clarity.

- Clarity means you know exactly where you're going and what you want. It's that simple.
- It REQUIRES that you have clear, hand-written (blue ink) goals on paper. (A format for goals is included later in this book.)

Before you can write your goals, it is necessary to write out a **Strategic Vision** for your life.

In order to write your Strategic Vision, you'll first need to write down 3 lists.

1. **Passion List**: write everything that you ever enjoyed doing or were passionate about, from early childhood until now.
2. **Competence List**: write everything that you were ever good at or felt you were good at, from early childhood until now.
3. **Don't Like List**: on a separate paper, write everything that you don't like doing, having or being, from early childhood until now.

Now, you have clarity about your passions, likes and dislikes! This way you can craft your strategic vision for maximum joy and satisfaction!

Your Strategic Vision must be written out as if already achieved - in present tense.

So what you can do is to position yourself in the future whether it's 1, 3, 5 or 10 years in the future - whatever feels right for you. Imagine that your life is fantastic. Now describe that. Pretend you're writing to your best friend. What does it look like? Smell like? Taste like? Sound like? Most importantly – FEEL LIKE?

(To ensure that your vision is congruent with your mental, physical, emotional and spiritual selves, do this: Read your vision, out loud, slowly to yourself many times. Feel for any sticking points, any points that don't feel wonderful. Cross out the word or phrase that is causing that and revise the vision in a way that feels awesome. Keep doing this until every word feels perfect. To fail to do this will ensure failure of your goal. Are you willing to do whatever it takes? It'll only take

about 20 minutes.)

Another good question is: "What would I need to do to not look back with regret?" Describe it in such detail that when you read it you get a giant smile on your face, your heart beats quickly and you get goose-bumps on your arms, you leap out of your chair and exclaim: **"YES - THIS IS EXACTLY WHAT I AM CREATING!"**

Here is the bottom line. To achieve the realization of your goals, you absolutely MUST "Get This". When I say "Get This", I mean really let it sink into the depths of your understanding.

1. There is hearing something and thinking you "got it".
2. There is believing you "got it"
3. There is knowing you "got it".
4. There is certainty in having "gotten it".
5. Then, there is having gotten it so completely that you live it moment by moment.

Knowing things intellectually is only the 1st level. You must put it into practice. One of the most insidious ego-traps is that it convinces you that you know something just because you've heard it before.

So, get this now and forever. You may think that you know this, but I am challenging you to really, honestly look inside and do whatever it takes to truly live this.

There are 10 primary reasons why people fail to achieve their goals.

---

1. They do not know exactly what they want.
2. They do not know exactly what they want.
3. They do not know exactly what they want.
4. They do not know exactly what they want.
5. They do not know exactly what they want.
6. They do not know exactly what they want.
7. They do not know exactly what they want.
8. They do not know exactly what they want.
9. They do not know the 2nd element of The Ultimate Success Formula.
10. They do not know the 3rd element of The Ultimate Success Formula.

It is so easy to say, *"of course I understand this!"* But you seriously don't. Please turn off your ego-mind for a moment and really feel into this. Your ego-mind is often your worst enemy. Do you really, really, really know exactly what you want, in all parts of you? You are physical, mental, emotional and spiritual. Are all parts in agreement with what you really want? Honestly look inside and see how often you are unclear about what you really want.

DO NOT continue reading until you have written out your 3 lists from a couple pages ago AND then written out your strategic vision from the previous page.

Seriously! Do not continue until you've done that!

The One BIG Thing:
Now, here's a huge clue to getting what you want. It is not taught in

any of the New Age LOA or manifesting books or programs but it **IS** taught in all of the ancient mystery school teachings. It's this:

> *Pick a single goal that you REALLY want right now*
> *and focus ONLY on that goal until it is achieved.*

I know we discussed goal-setting for every area of life, and that has its place. It's fine to consider and write down everything you want. Do the steps described and then **LET THEM ALL GO**. Put them out of your mind and forget about them. You have already communicated to the Universe/subconscious mind what you want (provided you felt huge passion as you wrote them). Let it handle the rest.

The **ONE BIG THING** goal is the one and only one you will continue to work with daily. This needs to be systematically impregnated into your subconscious mind, morning and night, via 5 minutes of extremely detailed visualization while still in your altered state. This visualization should include all 5 senses, be played as a present reality, and each time you revisit it - add more detail.

Ensure that every single element of your visualization is positive and happifying. Do this daily, first thing in the morning and last thing at night until the goal is achieved. You must be at complete ease about this because you KNOW it is a done deal, and feel exactly as if it is already realized. Be patient and confident. After each visualization, let it go from your conscious mind. Redirect your thinking to some super-happy memory and bask in the joy as you fall asleep or wake up.

Oh, one more thing. This also comes directly from the ancient mystery/occult teachings. Right before falling asleep and right after awakening, while still in the groggy (hypnotic) state, bring a clear vision of your One Big Goal into your mind, in the front of your head. As you hold it there in all its glory, move the image to the lower back of your skull and leave it there.

There is one more vital layer to your strategic vision that we'll discuss in the 3rd section. It has to do with **congruence**.

What did you learn from this chapter?

- Success is making continual progress toward your goals.
- You cannot get what you want until you know EXACTLY what you want.
- If you don't know what you want, you will get what other people want for you.
- Your chosen goals MUST be 100% authentic for YOU.
- Why successful people only do business with other successful people.
- Characteristics of successful people.
- You MUST have a written strategic vision!
- To write your vision, you'll need clarity on your passions, competencies and dislikes.
- Having clear, hand-written goals for every area of life almost assures achievement of those goals.
- Stop everything until you've written out your 3 lists and then your strategic vision.
- Create 1 BIG GOAL and focus on that am and pm via extremely detailed visualization until achieved.
- Only manifest 1 BIG goal at a time.

Element 2

Desire. Have you ever been underwater longer than was comfortable? Have you ever been underwater so long that you _desperately_ needed to get to the surface and get a breath? If you are fortunate enough to have had that experience, then you understand the level of DESIRE that is requisite to rapidly manifest anything. This is not "wishing" or "wanting", this is a "fire-in-the-belly", burning passion for your goal! You have to REALLY want it to the point of obsession.

Desire is the driver of manifestation. It is the energy, the impetus, the fuel. How much do you really, Really, REALLY want what you say you want? For most people most of the time the desire is not very strong. It is more of a wish or hope or a: _"this is what I think I would like"_ kind of thing. Worse yet, it is often something that a person thinks they <u>should</u> want. Well that simply isn't good enough to manifest your desires rapidly. You have to really, Really, REALLY want it! A burning desire is requisite.

So, how can you know whether you have the requisite level of desire? One useful criteria is to ask yourself: what am I willing to give up or sacrifice to get this? Am I willing to do whatever it takes to get this? How serious am I really, about having this? Are you willing to give up TV for 3 months? Going out? Drinking? Golf?

What do you do that you really like that you're willing to give up for a while? Is this goal more important than just about anything else? Am I willing to give up my loser friends and even family and only surround myself with positive people who are more successful than me? The answers to these questions will provide you with an accurate gauge of your level of desire.

Do you obsess about this goal day and night? Is it all-consuming?

Are things clicking into place in your consciousness now? Are you beginning to see why many of your goals have not been achieved?

If you're feeling quite uncomfortable now, and you're realizing that you actually don't have that level of desire for anything, and that you're comfortable as things are, then that's OK! You don't have to do anything. Did you write your passion list in the previous chapter? If not, then you may as well stop reading and resign yourself to ever more of the same. And that's OK. If you DID write your passion list, then surely you've rediscovered some things you really want.

Remember a few pages ago we discussed the One Big Goal? That comes from asking yourself: *"What is the ONE thing I want most right now?"* Do you have sufficient desire for it? You either do or don't. If you don't, then maybe you will discover it later. I suggest continuing to revise and expand your passion list.

Now, the stories I told in the previous section on Clarity apply here as well. For desire to be strong, the thing you want must be very honest and authentic for you. For example, most people say they want to be rich. But is that really true? They want to be rich because they think that is what they <u>should</u> want. Or more likely, they think being rich will give them what they really want which is freedom, satisfaction, happiness, fulfillment and high self-esteem.

Actually, more honestly, what they *really* want is the elimination of **pain** - the pain of working hard at a boring job or the pain of not working, the pain of being poor, the pain of having limited freedom, the pain of feeling hopeless, helpless and without self-determination, the pain of feeling undesirable, the pain of loneliness, the pain of feeling "less than", unsuccessful, unworthy, worthless, 2nd rate, stuck, trapped, etc.

The desire to eliminate pain is ABSOLUTELY different from the desire FOR a goal!

The desire to eliminate pain is a negative-goal. It is saying I DON'T want this. It is focusing on what you do not want. Therefore you will automatically create more pain! Pain-avoidance is not usually strong desire but it can be a turning point.

They each have completely different energy levels. So, clarity and desire are intermingled. Be very clear about this!

People (you) are driven to take any action by only two things.
1. The conscious pursuit of pleasure (5%).
2. The SUBconscious avoidance of pain (95%).

So, you, me and everybody else, mostly ***do anything because we***

believe, at a subconscious level, that action will reduce or eliminate a deep emotional pain.

This includes everything from the decision to hit the snooze button to whom to marry. Please ponder this a while. This is the secret to motivating people - including yourself! This is how you can get anyone to take any action.

Please re-read the previous paragraph now. And again! That is the secret to all human motivation. That is huge! This is a major golden nugget.

If you want to be rich, successful, happy, loved and healthy, you must hold massive desire for those things and that is the **OPPOSITE** of feeling frustration, anger, impatience, regret, etc. at NOT having those things now. This is a key point!

Now, the intense desire to remove your pain can be an important stepping stone. Feeling bored or complacent has a very low desire level and ensures nothing will change. Extreme frustration at your present circumstances is rousing and can break you out of complacency. When you get to the place of saying: *"I hate my life! I hate being poor, trapped, unsuccessful, unhappy, unsatisfied, unhealthy or unloved"*, that can be a major turning point. Then, what happens next is all important.

Desire feels completely different from wanting to eliminate the absence of something. 99% of people who say they want to be rich actually mean that they are sick and tired (pain) of feeling poor, restricted and unsuccessful. 1% of people are feeling happy and satisfied exactly where they are now and welcome more as well. THAT is exactly the mindset to become successful. This is key. The necessary state is to be in a state of **DESIRE without WANTING**. Wanting is feeling the absence of it. Wanting is separation from it. Desire must come from: *"I'm perfectly happy right here, right now AND wouldn't this other thing be fun also?"* You must feel exactly NOW, as you will when it shows up.

I know this feels contrary to the deep level of desire we discussed a few pages ago. And that is the Catch-22. How can you hold an intense desire for something yet still feel exactly as you will when it shows up? How can you desire something SO MUCH, yet be in a state of complete gratitude for it being already present?

We can call that: "Pre-Thanks".   We must come from a place of unity with that which we desire.

Use your emotional guidance system. We all have an inner guidance system that is continually telling us whether we are on track or off track. When you think about your goal, note how you feel. Do you feel elated, joyous, eager and expectant or do you feel the pain of not having it yet? Or more simply - do you feel good or bad?

Procrastination is frequently a by-product of a weak desire.

There is one more subtle but important distinction about desire types. Besides desire, there are compulsions, callings and destiny - whatever that means.

For example, I am a teacher. I HAVE to teach. It's what I am and what I must do. I call that a compulsion because it is never ultimately satisfying no matter how many raving testimonials, standing ovations or genuine hugs of gratitude I receive. I just have to teach. I often do it for free, I try to do it even when people don't want to learn and when I get a positive response it feels good, but only for an instant. That's a compulsion. Is that a calling or destiny? Sure, why not?

Your desire must be pure and powerful and congruent with all parts of you.

Now, remember that at the end of the previous chapter on Clarity, we discussed the necessity of manifesting 1 BIG Goal at a time? Well, that 1 Big Goal needs to be the thing you want most of all right now. It is the thing that you have maximum desire for. You can ask yourself: *"If I can only have 1 goal at a time, what do I want first?"*

"If your desire is strong enough, it doesn't matter what your beliefs are. If you have a desire that is strong enough, that desire will be the dominant vibration, and it will over-ride any other vibration that you have." ~ Abraham-Hicks

---

What did you learn from this chapter?

- Desire is the fuel of success.
- Desire must be far stronger than most people can muster.
- Desire must be authentic & congruent.
- Unconscious pain-avoidance drives 95% of human behaviour.
- Desire is opposite from pain-avoidance.
- Choose for your 1 BIG GOAL that which you desire most of all right now.
- How can you desire something SO MUCH, yet be in a state of complete gratitude for it being already present?

Element 3   •   # Certainty

Certainty is the third element in our ultimate success formula. Just like the other two elements, certainty is incredibly important. Certainty is closely tied into faith or belief. Obviously this is not a book on religion. However, many ancient religions do hold elements of Truth. Intrinsic to all historical religious texts and all true success teachings is the concept of faith.

Do you remember, in the previous section we discussed the Catch-22? *"How can you desire something SO MUCH, yet be in a state of complete gratitude for it being already present? "* That ties directly into certainty.

So what is faith anyway? Can we say that faith is believing in something that we can't yet see? Knowing that something is there even if we can't measure it or identify it or sense it with our five physical senses? That's probably as good a definition as any.

> *"**The key to manifesting my imagination is Knowing that it is already so. This is the Secret of the Ages!**"* ~ Abraham-Hicks

When we speak of certainty in regards to The Ultimate Success Formula, we're talking about ~~believing, knowing,~~ expecting our goal having been achieved already even though there is no physical evidence of it having manifested yet. This is exemplified by the book title by the late, great Wayne Dyer. He penned a book entitled, *"You'll See It When You Believe It"*. What a great title!

Now this is a very important and key piece right here. We can divide all of the people of the world into two groups.
1. Those who think they will believe it when they see it (99%), and
2. Those who know they will see it when they believe it (1%).

Group 1 are victims. They do not have control over their lives. They are not masters of their destiny. They will achieve few of their significant goals. These people continually think about and talk about what they do not want. They spend far less time thinking about what they do want. These people tend to blame, shame, regret, make excuses and are continual victims. This is 99% of humanity.

Group 2 is the small minority, the 1%. These are the people who are successful. These are the people who achieve most of their goals in a timely manner. These are the people who are masters of their destiny because they know with absolute certainty that what they truly believe will happen, happens. They take 100% responsibility for their life. They use the focus of their will - they direct their thoughts, they vibrate at a high level. They constantly focus on what they do want, and they spend very little time energy and emotion on what they do not want. They do not blame, shame, complain, regret, excuse or justify.

(Note: Some of these people are mis-guided, evil, a**-holes and use the same laws of the universe to create negative things. The universal laws do not judge, just like gravity works whether you're evil or good.)

So, in which group do you find yourself? In which group do you now CHOOSE to be? It's very important to differentiate between what you consciously think and what you subconsciously, actually and truly believe. Are you able to believe in things that you cannot see or measure? Well the fact is you do all day, every day. You can't see Wi-Fi or cell phone signals, and may not even have a clue how they work, yet you use them and believe in them.

Every morning when you get out of bed and put your feet on the floor you are believing that gravity is in effect and the floor is solid and will hold your weight, even though it is NOT true according to quantum physics. That is faith.

Faith is also driving on one side of a two-lane road with a single yellow line between the lanes and trusting that all of the other drivers going in the opposite direction will stay in their lane.

Have you ever driven on a country road in the dark? Your car's headlights only shine a few hundred feet. You cannot see any road beyond your headlights, yet you keep driving - TRUSTING that more road will appear.

So you see, you do have faith. You are fully capable of having faith in the unseen. So how much faith do you have that your goal will absolutely be achieved? How much certainty do you have that your goal will be achieved? An extremely high level of certainty is requisite for speedy manifestation of your goals!

"When you want something that you do not believe is possible, when you hold a desire for something that you do not expect - although a strong enough desire can override a weaker belief - it does not unfold easily, for you are not allowing it into your current experience."   ~Abraham-Hicks

"Pre-Thanks" is an easy habit to create to begin increasing your average certainty level. Let's say your goal is to increase your business revenue by 20%. Assuming that your Clarity is 7+, your Desire is 7+ and your Certainty is <7, you can say out loud to yourself: *"Thank you for the 20% increase in my business revenue! Thank you! Thank you! Thank you!"*   Better yet, do this first thing in the morning in front of your bathroom mirror while looking into your eyes and smiling and tapping your upper chest bone! Say this repeatedly for 5 minutes! Do so until you really FEEL it. Your feelings are your indicator on whether you are allowing the FLOW or pinching it off. (Please see addendum for full mirror process.)

What do you suppose will happen when you do this every morning for 5 minutes for 30 days? Are you willing to do whatever it takes? Is 5 minutes every morning too much to ask? How committed to your success are you?

"This place of knowing is a place of intense and incredible gratitude. It is thankfulness in advance. And that, perhaps, is the biggest key to creation: to be grateful before, and for, the

creation. Such taking for granted is not only condoned, but encouraged. It is the sure sign of mastery. All Masters know in advance that the deed has been done." [1]

Will you do it?

Self Esteem = 1st foundation of certainty. That is obvious, right? To have certainty in the successful outcome of a goal, we must have certainty in ourselves.

Worthiness = 2nd foundation of certainty. Worthiness is very different from self-esteem. While esteem has to do with our self-image of our intelligence, talents, attractiveness and skills and wisdom, worthiness is all about how we view the universe in which we live. Is it safe or dangerous? What was demonstrated to us as children? We'll cover this important point later in this book.

> *"What will building my Self-Esteem do for me? How you feel about yourself affects every aspect of your life. When your self-esteem is high, you are willing to take more risks, you can handle rejection easier, you take better care of yourself and you can achieve higher levels of peak performance. You can also facilitate this growth in others."* ~Jack Canfield.

Self esteem & worthiness are the product of your dominant subconscious beliefs. You will never transcend your dominant subconscious beliefs except temporarily through massive action or super-intense desire, as we discussed previously, OR permanently by

---

[1] *Neale Donald Walsch "Conversations With God"*

reprogramming your beliefs. The daily mirror self-talk ritual is one excellent way to permanently reprogram your subconscious beliefs. (Please see bonuses for full process.)

"Your Net-Worth will improve when your Self-Worth improves."
~Jim Rhon

So, how can you increase your level of certainty?

Pull out your strategic vision from chapter 1. You DID write one right?

If you did not, then you may as well quit right here because if you're unwilling to do a few simple exercises, your life will not change. Take a serious look at what self-sabotaging beliefs are causing this. FIX THEM NOW! 5 years from now, you will be 5 years older. Do you want to be the same person in 5 years or a master of your life? **Your decisions, right here, right now, are your point of power.**

"Your decisions will master you,
I whichever direction they take."[2]

If you did write out your strategic vision, then congratulations! Here's how to massage it to increase your level of certainty.

1. Get into a mentally quiet, meditative state by sitting comfortably with zero distractions (phone in non-disturb mode in another room). Breathe slowly and deeply for a while until you are calm.
2. Read your strategic vision out loud to yourself, slowly at least 10-20 times and notice ANY subtle resistance to any word or phrase in your strategic vision.

---

[2] Mary Baker Eddy, *"Science and Health with Key to the Scriptures."* P.392

3. Cross that word or phrase out.
4. Rewrite around that word or phrase in a way to eliminate the resistance.
5. Do this again and again.
6. That may require making your goals/vision smaller for a while until your comfort zone (set points) can catch up. You can expand your vision later. It's OK to revise it periodically. In fact, I encourage that.

When your strategic vision has zero resistance to you, then you KNOW your strategic vision is 100% congruent with all parts of you - your physical, mental, emotional and spiritual selves, and the 4 parts of your brain, and then having higher certainty will be so much easier.

In a later chapter, I'll discuss the unlimited power of pure belief. It will completely blow your mind - guaranteed.

The next way to increase your level of certainty is via using NLP, neuro-linguistic programming. This is much easier than it sounds. We all know that our facial expressions and body language reflect how we feel. When you are feeling down, deenergized, depressed, beaten down, or any such feelings, your face will be in a frown, your mouth will be slack, your jaw kind of loose, your shoulders slumped, your head forward and you will be breathing shallowly, and if you're walking, you'll kind of be shuffling.

You also know that when you are feeling on top of the world, you have a smile or grin or set look on your face, your jaw is firm, shoulders are back, chest out, you're breathing deeply, you stride with big strides, etc. Just think about the last time you felt on top of the world and it was your oyster. How was your face, your breathing, your body language?

Well, the really cool thing about NLP is that it works both ways. Yes, your body certainly reflects how you are feeling. Did you know that you can totally shift how you are feeling by putting your body into the body language position of an opposite state?

So if you want to feel empowered, confident, with high self esteem/worthiness, all you have to do is remember a time when you felt that way very, very strongly and pull up those feelings again and then stand like it, make your face like that, breath like that, and walk like you own the world. You will immediately start feeling that way. I'm sure you've heard the term: fake it till you make it? This is kind of what they're talking about. This is a very simple way to instantly shift your state of mind into an empowered one of confidence and certainty.

How would you like to anchor that into your subconscious mind permanently? Here's one way you can do it quickly and easily but it does take 5-10 minutes of mental work. Are you willing to do that? We're talking very short-term pain for a long-term gain.

So, here's how you do it. Remember that time when you felt totally empowered, totally self-confident, totally on top of the world, like the world was your oyster, you could do no wrong, you were in charge of the universe. Remember it fully. Recall every detail. Use all of your senses in your imagination. Take your time and bring up those feelings fully and completely. Adopt the body position and the facial position of that when you are fully feeling that. Next, imagine a large colored, geometric shape around you. It could be a big purple triangle, like a teepee. It could be a big orange ball, or any other shape or color that is big enough to totally surround you. While you are in the totally empowered state, simply put that shape and color around you. I'm going to call it a big orange ball. So, while you're in that state of total empowerment, you instantly imagine this big orange ball appearing around you. It's translucent so you can see through it. It's big and bright and it totally envelops you. It has a diameter of at least 6 feet and imagine it vividly. Now in your mind, associate the projection with your totally empowered State of Mind.

Next, relax and let the orange ball dissolve away. Then, put yourself back in that state of mind of total empowerment. As you are there, bring up the big orange ball again around you. Associate in your mind that orange ball with that state of total empowerment. Do this a number of times until your subconscious mind has totally connected and associated that big orange ball with that State of Mind of super empowerment. We can call it your Big Orange Super-Ball. Spend 10+ minutes doing this repeatedly. Don't short-change yourself. Really anchor that neuro-association through repetition.

From that time forward, anytime you want to feel that way again, simply imagine that big orange ball in front of you and then walk into it to instantly feel massively empowered. Isn't that a really cool, simple, and easy way to put yourself in Peak State immediately? If it doesn't work for you then you may need to re- anchor it.

Now, let's discuss your One BIG GOAL again. In order to manifest anything, we have to impregnate it into our subconscious mind. Your conscious mind decides what you want, and then you suggest the picture+feeling into your subconscious. Your subconscious is the manifesting mechanism - it makes it happen.

Let's say you (conscious mind) want an apple tree. You decide you want one. Then you plant the apple seed into the soil = you then plant it into your subconscious mind. Your subconscious then transforms that seed into a tree via magic. YOU are not the one creating the tree.

The process we described at the end of chapter 1, of detailed visualization am and pm, is how we create certainty. By faithfully performing the visualizations as described, daily, you will automagically attain the requisite level of certainty.

Commitment. What does that word mean to you?   When you commit to a goal, 100%, magic happens. Until you actually commit, there is hesitancy, there is Plan B, there is the chance of pulling back. That is doubt. That is the killer of certainty.

Do you recall hearing the story of the ancient army general who landed his forces on the beach of a superior enemy? He and his men knew they were out-numbered. So he ordered that all of their ships be burned. His soldiers now knew they either had to win or die, there was no retreat. That is commitment. And commitment creates certainty. They won.

The universal truth is that the moment you truly commit to a goal, all Creation moves to make it happen for and with you. Synchronicities will abound.

When you commit, then your Clarity is automatically very high, your Desire is automatically very high, and your Certainty is automatically very high. As you know by now, when all 3 are very high, then your goal is assured.

What did you learn from this chapter?

- Certainty is 100% faith.
- You will see it when you believe it.
- Belief is the foundation of all manifestation.
- Esteem and worthiness are different.
- Empowerment can be instantly worn via anchored association and NLP.
- "The key to manifesting my imagination is Knowing that it is already so. "
- Doing the daily visualizations on your 1 BIG GOAL will create certainty.
- Commitment is requisite and makes magic happen.

Elements All

Application, why use it, how to use it.

So there you have it, but you're not yet ready to use them! There are three elements to the ultimate success formula. Now the trick is in using them correctly. Their proper application means everything.

These three elements are what is necessary to achieve your dreams and goals and aspirations. If you have a very clear goal and you really want it and you know it's going to be achieved, you WILL - with mathematical precision, achieve that goal. Eventually. So now the big question is, how long will it take? Well that depends on the level of each 3.

For each goal, we need to evaluate ourselves on a scale of 1 to 10, with 1 being the lowest level and 10 being the highest possible level.

1. So I'd like you to get a piece of paper and a pen right now and stop until you have that in front of you.
2. Next, write down one of your major goals.
3. Now look at that goal and ask yourself: "on a scale of 1 to 10, how high is my level of Clarity?"
4. Please carefully reread the section on "Clarity" so that you truly understand what that exactly means. Details are important.
5. So how high is your Clarity, on a scale of 1 to 10?

Here is what that can look like:

Goal	Clarity	Desire	Certainty	Rectification
Write your goal as an already-accomplished fact (past-tense). Be specific, measurable, attainable, realistic and timely.	On a scale of 1-10, how high is your Clarity for this goal?	On a scale of 1-10, how high is your Desire for this goal?	On a scale of 1-10, how high is your Certainty for this goal?	What can I do to raise the low ones?
1-				
2-				
3-				
4-				
5-				

Next do the same thing with Desire. On a scale of 1 to 10, how intense is your desire?

Now Certainty. On a scale of 1 to 10, how absolute is your certainty?

If you can honestly rate yourself at a level 8 or above on all three, then you can be assured that your goal will manifest in a reasonably short period of time. The closer you are to 10 on all of them, the faster your goal will manifest. If you are below 7 on any of them, then you have some work to do. Or you may need to revise or drop that goal.

So now let's consider some of the goals you have that haven't been achieved or seem to be taking too long.

Write each one out on a piece of paper (like the grid I showed above) and then rate it on a scale of 1 to 10 for clarity, desire, and certainty. Be sure to be very honest with yourself.

You cannot fool yourself - I know, I've tried and I know you have also.

See which one of the three elements you rated below level 7 for each of your goals. Now you know exactly what you need to do to achieve that goal.

So do you see how incredibly useful and functional this success formula is? This becomes very easy to use, simple to understand methodology or benchmark with which to evaluate all of your goals. This puts you in the driver's seat. This makes life much simpler to understand. This gives you a clear understanding of how to get what you want, and a clear understanding of why you haven't gotten everything you wanted.

But, even though this tool is super-simple, it doesn't mean it is easy to use. You still have to rate yourself honestly on each element for each major goal and then do the work necessary to get above 8. We're not done yet!

Clarity+Desire+Certainty=Success!

What did you learn from this chapter?

- How exactly, to use the formula.
- It is a benchmark.
- It shows exactly why past goals have not manifested.
- It points to exactly what to do to manifest those goals.
- We're not done yet!

Chapter 5: BUT WHAT ABOUT MASSIVE ACTION?

If you've been paying attention, you're likely asking about the missing ingredient of massive action.

So many success "gurus" and books promote "massive action" as the big key to success. How often have you read or heard someone being interviewed about the reason for their success, and them giving the answer: "Hard work!"? Why  do they say that? Usually because they are actually not consciously aware of the fact that their dominant subconscious beliefs are the causative factor. Yet I've omitted massive action from the Ultimate Success Formula. Here's why:

Action is not a cause of success - it is an effect of Clarity+Desire+Certainty.

Action is the conduit by which Clarity+Desire+Certainty are expressed. When your Clarity+Desire+Certainty are all above 8/10, then you WILL take all necessary action almost without effort! Even more importantly, your actions will be INSPIRED! Inspired action is always efficient and effective and doesn't feel like work, while uninspired action is wasted energy, time and resources.

*"What is the definition of procrastination? It means:
I can feel within my Energy sensor that this action is not in
perfect alignment at this time."* ~ Abraham/Hicks

Kevin Trudeau, in his audio series: *"Your Wish IS Your Command"*, discusses the "Training-Balance Scale". This is a scale of action vs. thought. At one end of the scale we have massive action, doing, doing, and doing some more. This is rooted in the belief that you have to work very hard to be successful, that money is difficult to make, that we have to earn our living.

At the other end, we have thought, emotion and feeling. The conventional theories push that we need a balance of the two to be successful. Kevin (and all masters) calls BS. Success is 99.9% thought, emotion, feeling. Success is mental!

The Universe is Mental!

Success is the mental imprint of what you really want onto the vast blanket of pure potentiality (the implicate order). Then, potential is quantified (per quantum physics - waves into particles) into 3D "reality", *usually VIA action.*

So, action can be extremely important, and almost always is necessary for the unfoldment, the expression, the manifestation of your clarity, desire and certainty. Action is the conduit for the success in the 3D world, but it is not the driver of success, because success is a 5D manifestation.

When your clarity, desire and certainty are all high, then synchronicities will automagically happen and intuitive guidance will become apparent, but you MUST ACT on those immediately, with full faith and trust. Then, your actions will be maximally productive. This is very different from "massive action" which is blind.

Massive action - benefits and limitations:

1. It can override limiting subconscious beliefs because massive action carries a HUGE amount of energy. If not, it isn't MASSIVE action - merely action.
2. It is hit or miss. If you throw enough wet spaghetti at the wall, some of it will stick eventually. If enough massive action is applied for a long enough time, then successes will occur due to the cyclic nature of everything. You know how one popular definition for "luck" is: "When preparation meets opportunity?" Well, what you don't realize is that opportunity is cyclical. If you are doing massive action all the time, then your preparation will meet opportunity WHEN that cycle comes around again. But that is a hugely inefficient way to progress.

When you take **_INSPIRED_** action, it will be at the correct time of the cycle for that endeavour, and therefore, effective. Inspiration flows when your Clarity+Desire+Certainty are very high.

So, should you take action? Yes, but only when inspired and only after your Clarity+Desire+Certainty are each above 8/10.

Will you take action? Yes, most likely, to the degree that you believe that massive action is necessary.

"Take the time to line up the Energy first, and action becomes inconsequential. If you don't take the time to line up the Energy, if you don't find the feeling place of what you're looking for, not enough action in the world will make any difference."[3]
~ Abraham/Hicks

The billionaires and multi millionaires go to work every day and seem to work hard and play hard. Why? Do you think it is because they LOVE what they do and don't consider it work?

Do you know what else all the billionaires and multi millionaires have in common? They are all highly intuitive! Yes, seriously! Many of them always carry around little notebooks where they immediately write down their intuitive hits. Then they implement (act on) those hits as soon as possible. They always act on their intuitive hits ASAP, and never act without an intuitive hit. The most famous is Leonardo, whose notebooks are famous and almost priceless.

We all have 3 decision centers: head, heart and gut. (Note: some people reverse the heart & gut as explained below).

Our head sources intellectual decisions. The problem here is that we cannot possibly have all relevant knowledge and there will always be hidden variables. Some head decisions are good because they are data-driven which is good for some sorts of decisions, like market

---

[3] https://www.facebook.com/Abraham.Hicks/posts/333331460126849

research, some science, actuarial, and accounting. But our intellect is fundamentally handicapped because:

1. It is based in the past. Intellect cannot predict the future. Good decisions MUST anticipate the future.
2. Intellect can never access all relevant data.
3. Intellect can never anticipate all relevant variables.

Consider all of your head-based decisions. What is their success rate? Not so good, right?

Our heart produces emotion-based decisions. These are usually wrong. Think about your emotion-based decisions. What is their success rate? Rather dismal, right? The two primary emotions are greed and fear. Any decision based on greed or fear is bound to be a bad decision (except for matters of physical survival).

Our gut is a term for intuitive decisions. If you will take some time to reflect on the successes in your life, you will see that they were all due to listening and acting on your intuitive guidance. When you reflect on the failures in your life, you will see that they were all due to ignoring your intuitive guidance! Please do this now. It is important.

Here's how:

1. Write down 3 significant success in your life.
2. For each, consider the big decision you made prior to that success that caused that success.
3. Now, for each one consider the intuitive hit that gave you that big decision. Each big decision you made that led to a big success came from an intuitive hit.

4. Consider that process or mechanism.
    a. How did you know it was an intuitive hit?
    b. What did it sound like or feel like? See if you can clearly identify how it is that your intuition speaks to you in a way that you know and recognize it.
5. When you can do that, then you really have a magical genie at your beck and call.

Do this same process for three of your big failures. You will note that for each one, you did get an intuitive hit but you hesitated, and then you let your head or heart take over and screw it up for you because your decision ended up being based on your intellect or an emotional fear.

So here is a powerful little test. Without thinking about it, immediately answer the following question with the first number that pops in.

On a scale of 1 - 10, how intuitive are you? Write down that number. This is your level of ability to quickly recognize when you are actually getting intuitive guidance (or hits) and can differentiate it from other noise like thoughts, emotions, programming or other people's words in your head.

Intuition is very quiet - much quieter than the noise we just mentioned. Consider your successes again and see if you can remember the intuitive "hit" that gave you the right direction or answer. What did that feel like? Was it a feeling in your body? Was it a voice? Was it a quiet knowing? How does your intuition speak to you? When you identify this, it will instantly make you far more intuitive! How intuitive are you now?

Here's the second question. Answer the following question with the first number that pops in. On a scale of 1 - 10, how often and quickly do you <u>immediately</u> act on your intuition? Write down that number. What is it? Is it close to 10? Is it well below 10? Of course it is a low number, otherwise you wouldn't be reading this book because you wouldn't need it!

If your life is not nearly as successful as you wish it to be than your intuitive ability is below 7 and/or your speed of implementation is below 7. I've coached over 3,300 entrepreneurs and business people from 47 countries and always got consistent responses. Your level of success is dependant on your intuitive ability AND speed of implementation being above 7/10.

OK, you already know that your intuition always tells you the right decision, provides the right information you need when you need it, and always tells you the next right step to take. Right?

So why in the hell aren't you working to be better at recognizing your intuition?

Why don't you instantly act on your intuition 100% of the time with 100% blind faith?

Stop right now and answer that clearly, on paper, for yourself. Seriously!

(If you didn't stop and do that, then you have some serious self-sabotaging subconscious beliefs that are directly preventing your living in the flow. Your life will not improve until you handle and reframe those. Did what I just say trigger you? Did it tick you off? Did your ego jump in with both feet and say: I know this?)

What do you suppose will happen when you boost your ability to recognize your intuition to a 9/10 AND you act on it as soon as possible at least 90% of the time?

> Will your life become harder or easier?
> Will your life become less fun or more fun?
> Will your life become less productive or more productive?
> Will you become less successful or more successful?
> Will you reach your goals slowly or much faster?

You now know exactly what to do to live in the flow most of the time. I know you know what living in the flow is like and what it means. And I know you love it when it happens. Would you like to live in the flow most of the time? Now you know exactly how to do that. Isn't that awesome and amazing? Are you going to do it?

I love this brilliant quote from the super, mega-successful Jack Canfield (*co-author of the world-wide best selling "Chicken Soup for the Soul" series.*)

"I have achieved an enormous amount of success in my life, and I owe it all to two things:
- The first is that I have learned how to access my intuition

and tune into my inner guidance,
which comes from both my own subconscious mind
and the Higher Power that created this Universe
<u>and wants us to thrive.</u>
I have learned how to meditate, use guided visualization,
and read the kinesthetic signals from my body
(what some people call "trusting your gut feeling").
- The second is that I have learned to take immediate action
on my inner guidance—the quicker, the better!"[4] ~ *Jack Canfield*

Now, are you ready to have your mind blown?

If you worked 8 hours/day for 50 weeks (1 work year), that would be 2,000 hours of work. If you devoted 2,000 hours of work toward 1 goal of yours, how much progress would that provide? You'd likely make a lot of progress toward your goal.

Now, consider this:

> *"17 seconds of pure-belief is equal to 2,000 man action hours."*
> ~Abraham/Hicks.

Seriously: "17 seconds of pure-belief is equal to 2,000 man action hours." That doesn't blow your mind? Try this one:

> *"68 seconds of pure-belief is equal to*
> *2 million man action hours."*
> ~Abraham/Hicks.

Can you wrap your head around that? Remember, the universe is

---

4

https://www.jackcanfield.com/blog/the-secret-to-achieving-your-biggest-goals-and-dreams/

mental! Matter is a mere, temporary by-product of clear and powerful intention with belief (Clarity+Desire+Certainty).

How much progress could you make toward your goal with 2 million man-action hours of work? That's 1,000 years of work!

Of course, this isn't anywhere as easy as it sounds. The kicker is "pure belief". That includes and is predicated on staying focused on a single thought for 17 seconds, or staying on a pure stream of congruent thoughts. Can you do that? With Pure Belief? With absolutely zero doubt or resistance?

Try this: Have a watch or clock with a second hand (or phone), look at the time, close your eyes and focus on 1 single thought until another aberrant thought intrudes. Immediately open your eyes and note the seconds. Typically, people can focus on a single thought for an average of 3 seconds when they really try and practise. How can we have pure belief when we can't even focus on a single thought for a few seconds? This is worth practising, right?

You know whether you're on track by how you feel. If you can focus on your desire (via detailed, multi-sensory visualization) and feel really awesome about it for 17+ seconds, you've got the key! Then just string together 4 sets of 17 seconds.

The good news is this:

1. You now know an incredibly amazing piece of information that

can skyrocket your success and speed it up to an astounding degree.

2. The requisite skills can be learned via practise.

Would you rather work your butt off working thousands of hours on achieving your goals OR work your brain off developing the skill of pure focus with pure belief so that you can easily keep creating at will?

The hardest work in the world is to be able to consistently focus one's thought. It is also the #1 requisite skill for any type of success.

Now what do you think about massive action?

What did you learn from this chapter?

- Action is an effect, not a cause.
- Massive action vs. inspired action.
- The training-balance scale.
- The universe is mental.
- The intuition secret weapon.
- How to live in the flow.
- The astounding power of sustained pure belief.

www.SuccessTiming.com

"Always Start with The End in Mind!"

Metaphysical Philanthropist: Marcus Geier & MoonCoach: Silvia Pancaro

Chapter 6: "What" + "Why" vs. "How"?

You've likely heard people say that the quality of your answers depends on the quality of your questions. Have you? So, what are the best questions?

Successful people are strategic - focused on the **WHAT** and the **WHY**. What do you really want and why do you want it? They do not ever sweat the **HOW**.

Here's a story to illustrate. You've likely been this person and seen such people numerous times.

Imagine your friend Suzy, comes running up to you all excited, bouncing with energy, unable to contain her excitement and enthusiasm. She excitedly tells you: "I'm so happy, I'm so excited, I'm so enthused, I got this great idea! I'm going to do/create/start [insert awesome idea here] and it's going to be awesome!" Her face is lit up like a supernova and she has a huge smile on her face and she can't contain the amount of energy running through her body. And then, all of a sudden, her face drops, her energy drops, her shoulders slump, her pure joy turns into sadness, and she says something like: "but I don't know HOW I'm going to do this or I don't know HOW I'm going to get the money to do this."

Is that familiar? Have you been this person? Yes you have, likely many times.

Let's look at this and learn from it okay? In the first portion, your friend (or you) were focused on the WHAT with a powerful WHY. Your friend was focused on the project or the idea or the plan that was just so all-encompassing and exciting that her entire face and body language spoke volumes about the super-high level of energy.

At that moment, your friend was powerfully manifesting that vision into 3D reality via the law of resonance. The entire universe was conspiring to bring that into physical manifestation. Your friend had extremely high Clarity, Desire, and Certainty. Would you agree that your friend's Clarity was pegged at 10 out of 10? Her desire was also at a 10 out of 10? And her certainty was at a 10 out of 10?

Then what happened? Their/your focus switched to the HOW. "How am I going to do this? How am I going to get the money?" The HOW is not their job. They must stay absolutely focused on the WHAT with a powerfully compelling WHY. That is how it works.

As soon as they switched their focus from the WHAT and WHY to the HOW, their energy completely dropped to close to zero. They were actually in a state close to depression. What is the result of that? The Universe immediately stopped all progress to bring that dream goal or situation into manifestation. Why? Because the clarity was still high, but the desire was completely dissipated due to a total drop in certainty. The desire dropped to 5 and the certainty went down to zero. We cannot maintain a high desire for anything if there is no certainty that it is achievable. That's pretty clear right?

So, the focus is all important. And the quality of the focus is evidenced by the emotional guidance system.

In the first part, when your friend was totally focused on the WHAT with a powerfully compelling WHY, they felt awesome. They felt empowered, happy, joyful, excited, on top of the world, unstoppable. Those are all highly positive emotions. Then when their focus switched to the HOW, their energy dropped and they felt depressed, discouraged, frustrated, angry, anxious, fearful, powerless! Those are all negative emotions.

So do you see how your emotional state is an indicator of the quality and focus of your thinking?

Your TO DO list. Please get your notebook and pen out again. Let's do a little to-do list. Draw a vertical line down the middle of the paper. Entitle the left column: "My To Dos". Entitle the right column: "Universe To Dos". In the left column, write your goal - the WHAT and the WHY. Now, anything that has to do with the HOW goes into the right column. The only time you act on a to-do item is immediately following an intuitive "hit" that you should do so. Until that happens, sit back, relax KNOWING that the entire universe is working furiously to bring into reality what you declared you want with high clarity, high desire and high certainty.

My To Do (What + Why?)	Universe To Do (the HOW)
1.	1.
2.	2.
3.	3.
4.	4.

Your job is to stay focused on the WHAT. The Universe's job is to manage the millions of little actions necessary to handle the HOW. *(Thanks to Burge Smith Lyons, CEO of EssenceOfBeing.com).* It will do this via synchronicities and via intuitive hits to you about what action to take next. Do those as soon as possible. Then, your job is to stay out of the universe's way (resist doubt) and ALLOW, with very high clarity, desire and certainty. Your doubt, anxiety and muddied thinking will block the manifestation. Stay clear.

"The root of all evil - is doubt." ~ *Marcus Geier*

How you think is infinitely more important that what you do, or say.

"Whether you believe you can do a thing or not, you are right."
~ *Henry Ford*

How do you know if you are allowing or blocking? Simply by how you feel.

> When you feel bad - you are blocking.
> When you feel bad - you are focused on what you do NOT want - the HOW.
> When you feel bad - you are literally creating what you do not want!
> That's why you feel bad.

When you feel good - you are allowing.

When you feel good - you are focused on what you DO want - the WHAT & WHY.

When you feel good - you are literally creating what you DO want!

That's why you feel good.

It is simple. It is not easy because it requires the hardest work in the world - focusing your thoughts! Mental discipline! That is exactly why meditation is so important. Meditation is the practice of gaining awareness and control over our ego-mind so that we may purposefully direct our focus. Why do you think we are surrounded with distractions? The powers that were don't want us to focus the tremendous power of our thoughts!

"When you talk about what you want and why you want it, there's usually less resistance within you than when you talk about what you want and how you're going to get it. When you pose questions you don't have answers for, like how, where, when, who, it sets up a contradictory vibration that slows everything down." ~ Esther Hicks

What did you learn from this chapter?

- Strategic thinking for success.
- What & Why vs. How.
- Your emotional guidance system.

What do you REALLY want? WHY?

Chapter 7: The Secret to To Do Lists

TO DO lists are important. Whether you are taking massive action, inspired action or 68 seconds of pure belief, your results will generally come by way of action (until you truly master conscious, sustained focus). Most people struggle with To Do lists. They either don't make them (always write your list the evening before, and Sunday evening before the week) or they don't use them consistently. This is not a time management book, that's a whole other book, but I see the same struggles from many of my coaching clients.

The secret to an effective To Do list (besides good prioritization) is that To Do items must be small enough.

Are you procrastinating on your list? Is there resistance to getting them done? Frequently, that is due to your To Do items actually being multi-step projects (like update your website, write a blog article, write a proposal, revamp your social media pages, etc.) Those are all projects, not To Do items.

Let me illustrate. I've had the goal of working out at the gym 3 times/week for decades now. I'd do ok for a few months, then stop for a few months. I realized that I had significant resistance to that goal. It doesn't matter why.

So I reframed my goal into 4 goals - each a single-action item.
   1. Get up at 6am 3 days/week.

2. *Put on my gym clothes.*
3. *Drive to the gym.*
4. *Walk inside.*

I had no internal resistance to any of those 4 goals.
Motivation/discipline problem solved.

So, if your To Do list says: "update my website", you may look at that in the morning and think to yourself: *"Well, to do that I need to figure out my target markets, determine their primary subconscious pain points, write a core marketing message to evoke a subconscious sigh of relief, find the right subliminal pictures, go to Fiverr and get illustrations made, do some research for the stats I need to put up, email 5 clients for their testimonials, determine the appropriate marketing channels, etc., etc., etc. I'm way too busy for all of that today, I'll do it next week."* Boom! We have procrastination - the killer of productivity.

Instead, break down your project into single-action items that can be done in a few minutes with little thought or planning. Using the "update my website" example: what are the small steps needed to accomplish that?

1. Revisit who exactly my target markets are.
2. Have I correctly identified the primary pain points for each target?
3. Summarize the pain points that I wish to address.
4. Revise my core marketing messages for each pain point.
5. Summarize that into a single sentence or two.
6. Identify where/how to place that message near the top of my 1st page.
7. Ensure it is compelling.

8. Ensure that the 1st page (top) makes viewers feel unconsciously safe and tusting.
9. Ensure that they get the core marketing message instantly.
10. Ensure that they get the core marketing message is directly relevant to their pain.
11. Ensure that the core marketing message instantly evokes a giant subconscious sigh of relief.
12. etc.

That way, whenever you have a few minutes, you can check your list and find something you can complete right then and there. Progress made!

Always look for ways to reduce resistance. Resistance is a message that something is out of whack (congruence). Remember, we are physical, intellectual, emotional and spiritual. All parts must be in congruence or you have resistance. Stop and fix it.

What did you learn from this chapter?

- To Do lists are valuable.
- To Do items must be small, single action items.
- Always analyze and remove resistance.

Alex Beattie

Chapter 8: The Essential 5D - How Life Really Works

We all (people on this planet currently), are moving from 3D to 5D. This is affecting how we do business going forward, how we do relationships and how we do health. It is all changing very quickly at a core level. This is a function of the end of the 26,000 year astronomical cycle (typically called the precession of the equinoxes) and is effected via vastly increased and altered energy hitting us through the sun. That is what is driving climate change (not man-created CO_2) and economic and demographic cycles. The fact that all of the planets and moons in our solar system have been undergoing massive climate change over the past 50+ years is enough to resoundingly disprove man-made climate change.

A single, large volcanic eruption can alter the world's climate more in one month than all human action combined. The entire basis of man-induced climate change derives from a single CO_2 model - the so-called "hockey puck" graph of historical CO_2 levels. That model has been completely debunked, even by its creator who admitted to its fraud! I could on but we won't discuss this further here, but there is plenty of material explaining and proving this, such as the excellent works of David Wilcock & Martin Armstrong.

Next, consider that whatever agenda the world's governments and all mainstream media are pushing collectively is always the opposite of the truth and has an insidious hidden purpose. 100%. In this case, it is to add another huge layer of taxes onto humanity to move even more wealth from the many to the few via carbon taxes.

So, why did I rant about climate change there? It is an example of conditioning that is imposed on us and for which we must be on guard. Always. Question your beliefs! ALL OF THEM!

One of the big false programs educated into us is that 3D, the world of Newtonian Physics, the material world of physicality and linear time, is the truth about reality. It is what we all learned in science class in grade school, based on the "fact" that matter is solid and reacts to matter around it. Matter, we were taught, is fixed, real, solid, and the ultimate reality. 3D is the world where we are born, helpless and ignorant, and we have to grow up slowly, learn tremendous amounts of education, get a "good" job, make money, pay bills, buy a house and two cars, fall in love, get married with an expensive wedding, have kids, raise them the same way we were raised with our limiting beliefs, fears and judgments, pay massive debt, retire, grow old while deteriorating and die.

3D is the world of traditional allopathic medicine dogma (treat symptoms, not causes). Our bodies are machines made up of disparate parts and if one is broken, fix it via poisoning (drugs or radiation) or surgery. 3D is the world of corporatism and the politics that corporations manage, and private central banking. Obviously, 3D is a horrific way to live! It is slavery. So stop it! There's a better way!

4D is a transitional state and not really pertinent to this discussion. It is like our dream state. It is a mental dimension filled with a lot of good and not so good garbage.

5D is the beginning of metaphysics, the level of consciousness that understands that all is connected energy, is nonlinear (time and space) and exists as pure potentiality. Space is an illusion, as is linear time. Please stop and consider this.

5D is the world of quantum physics. The observer effect is all-important here. Since everything exists as pure potentiality (the implicate order), we can create anything (the explicate order) at any time via pure focus. A good analogy is the replicator machines in Star Trek. The replicators use energy, and create anything on demand from a stored blueprint or pattern. Also, the holodeck in Star Trek is a most useful analogy.

By now, countless scientific experiments have proven that matter is not solid and is created and dis-created on demand, all of the time. Everything is continually switching between wave (energy) and particle (matter). You create your reality on a continuous basis via your observation (expectation).

(There is a huge body of knowledge fully explaining all of this). For a

really fun primer, watch the movie: "What the Bleep do We know - Down the Rabbit Hole", but watch "The Secret" first, and study the works of people like David Wilcock, Lynn McTaggart & Dr. Joe Dispenza).

Your brain, and heart and gut think thoughts and send them out continuously. Thoughts are measurable EMF waves. They necessarily affect (and effect) everything they contact. Focused thought (via intention), power and continuity, create matter (flip waves into particles).

So, according to quantum physics, and all ancient esoteric teachings (mystery schools), YOU create your life 100% of the time. So far, you've been doing so largely by default, unconsciously in alignment with your dominant subconscious beliefs. Now it is time to start creating your life deliberately and consciously. How? Easy! Use "The Ultimate Success Formula!"

(Note: another layer involves the theory that we (as our Higher Selves) pre-determine a series of life-events and circumstances prior to incarnation. So, we all can't be kings, queens, presidents, billionaires or Elvis because we didn't pre-choose that. Fortunately, all of those things we authentically desire are within our pre-chosen experience array.)

You are thinking thoughts all the time. Psychologists tell us that over 90% of our thoughts are the same as we thought yesterday. These are thought-habits that come from our subconscious beliefs. They are unfocused and are creating a wide array of seemingly random life-effects because your entire life experience is the effect, or out-picturing or manifestation of your dominant thoughts.

***Your dominant thoughts literally create your entire reality.
100%.***

Therefore, the better you get at focusing/directing your dominant thoughts, the more your life experience will conform to those!

How do you know whether you are on track or off-track? By your emotions. Are you feeling good or bad. I know we touched on this in a previous chapter, but it is vital to really "get" this. Notice, throughout your day, whether you're feeling good or bad. That is your indication of whether you are actively creating what you want or what you don't want. You are always creating - as long as you are thinking - you are creating! By being disciplined in your thinking, you will create ever more of what you want and ever less of what you don't. The intensity of desire is the fuel. See, it's simple.

So what do you want? What do YOU really, Really, REALLY want?
>   To feel happy?
>   To feel satisfied?

Isn't that ultimately what you really want? The ultimate success?

Well, here's the code:

Happiness = Gratitude!
Satisfaction comes from service!

There you have it!

What did you learn from this chapter?

- 3D sucks. 5D is where it's at.
- Your thoughts literally create your experience. 100%.
- Emotional guidance system.
- How to be happy and satisfied.

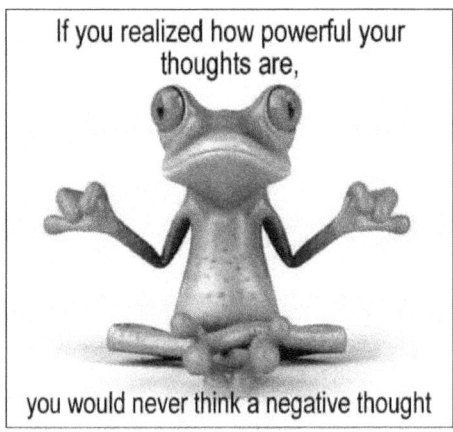

If you realized how powerful your thoughts are,

you would never think a negative thought

www.thequotepedia.com

Chapter 9: Practical 5D

What can we conclude from this? We can work, do, work and do some more. How has that been working out for you? How functional has that been for all of those "hard workers" out there? Or, we can relax into the stream of all well-being after we have impregnated the field of all potentiality with our clear order and then take guided, inspired action. THAT is living in the FLOW.

Have you ever heard the term: PRONOID? It is the opposite of paranoid.

1. Paranoid is the core belief that the universe is out to get you.
2. Pronoid is the core belief that the universe is out to help you!

You get to choose! You can only be one or the other. Let's choose to be pronoid! Always!

> **"I think the most important question facing humanity is,**
> **'Is the universe a friendly place?'**
> **This is the first and most basic question**
> **all people must answer for themselves."** ~ *Albert Einstein*

The favorite mantra of the wildly successful is a version of:

> **'Even though I have no idea how,**
> **I know that everything is working out brilliantly for me!'**

This means that we KNOW wonderful things are happening despite not being able to see them. It means that no matter the catastrophe, there is a huge blessing coming. That is faith, belief, certainty! How about writing that on sticky notes and placing them all around your home, car and office?

So, let's say that you're living your life and all of a sudden you get whammied by a disaster. It could be a bad car accident, a financial collapse, losing your job, business failure, spouse cheats on you or a major health crisis.

Why did this happen "to" you? It happened because you were vibrating thoughts around the level of the "bad" experience. You may have been feeling depressed, or unforgiving of someone, yourself or some situation, or feeling insecure, worrying, or any number of focuses. It could be a very low-level focus (like guilt or anxiety or depression), something you're not really consciously aware of because you've been engaging in some sort of avoidance mechanism, usually an addiction of some sort.

Do you react or respond? Reacting is from your old programming. You can feel devastated, confused, scared, angry, shaken, insecure, depressed. What will happen should you decide to react this way? You will create more of it!

Or you could respond with:

"Even though I have no idea how,
I KNOW that everything is working out brilliantly for me!"

And then truly relax and deeply trust (and laugh). 100%.

How can we say this in response to a disaster?

1. We can because we KNOW that the universe is out to help us. Because we KNOW our dominant thoughts create our reality. Because as soon as we redirect our thoughts toward what we want, as evidenced by feeling good, our experience will heal and this disaster will be turned into a blessing in a completely unknown, surprising way.

2. We can because we know that our conscious mind (who we think we are) is only a very small part of us. We are spiritual (energy) beings who have chosen to temporarily forget who we really are in order to experience contrast to more fully understand our magnificence as extensions of Source Energy. You are NOT your body and ego-mind! They are just avatars so that you can fit into and interact with this video game we call life. So this disaster, that seems so big and terrible is actually a tiny blip in the context of our total reality and ultimately will be seen as merely just another experience, like watching a scene in a movie.

Please write that sentence on sticky notes and place them all around your home, car and office!

"I KNOW that everything is working out brilliantly FOR me,
even if I have no idea HOW!"

Let THAT become your default response via practice. Your life will transform!

What did you learn from this chapter?

- Be Pronoid
- Respond, don't react
- Your new mantra
- You are much bigger than you think.

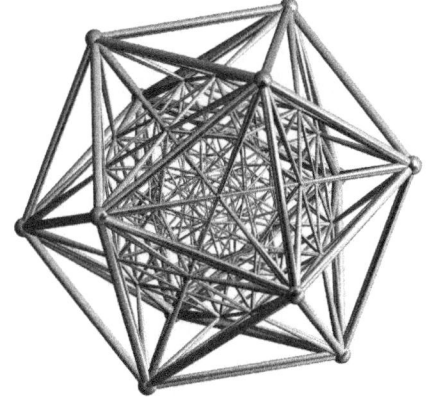

Chapter 10: Conclusion

We have discussed how life works and you either are familiar with quantum physics or not. If not, then what we have presented here may seem far-fetched and difficult to accept. Of course this is the case because we provided minimal explanation. Please do some research into quantum physics and how it affects your life.

Again, for a really fun primer, watch the movie: *"What the Bleep do We know - Down the Rabbit Hole"*, (but watch *"The Secret"* first). In fact, I highly recommend watching each several times.

If you are versed in quantum physics, 5D and Law of Attraction, then surely you now have a more clear, simple and functional understanding that you can really use on a daily basis to achieve any goal.

The Ultimate Success Formula is a uniquely useable tool and a benchmark. I hope that you will create the simple chart from Chapter 4, and use it to analyze all of your goals. Then, check in with the chart daily to see where you are on your goals.

The really exciting news it that YOU are 100% in charge of creating YOUR life any way you want! All you need to do is:

1. Be crystal clear on what you want,
2. Have an intense desire/passion for it,
3. KNOW it is coming to you!
4. Then, feel good all of the time so that you are in the receptive state and can hear your intuition that will tell you HOW or what actions to take
5. Then always ACT on your intuitive hits immediately.
6. Never doubt!

I know that when you really internalize this and apply it continuously, you will quickly start living the life of your dreams! But...this is powerful stuff!

I'm sure you've heard the old saying: "Be careful what you wish for, you might get it!" Be careful when setting goals. If you want a life of ultimate satisfaction and fulfillment, a life that you won't later regret, a life of joy, then ensure that your goals do good in the world. Also, choose goals that will get you the FEELINGS you're actually after, not just the things that you may believe will get you what you really want.

Service to self is the path to misery.
Service to others is the path to satisfaction.

Choose wisely!

May you choose to focus the universal energy in directions that will bring you peace, joy, satisfaction and fulfillment and bless everyone and everything.

I appreciate you!

Congratulations for doing this for yourself (and the planet)!

Marcus Geier

(see below for your bonuses!)

Bonus 1: How to stop all stress and solve any problem.

Here is how to release all stress and solve all problems in about 3-10 minutes per problem

1. Get paper and pen and find somewhere quiet and distraction-free.
2. Write down a problem statement. What is 1 problem that is stressing you? Write it down. I.e.: "*I don't know how I'm going to pay my bills.*"
3. Write down as many possible solutions you can think of. Write as many as you can, even bad/crazy/bizarre/unrealistic solutions. Don't think about whether they are good solutions or not.
4. Looking at your paper, sit comfortably, relax, do some slow, deep breathing, close your eyes halfway and get into a meditative state. Keep breathing until you are relaxed.
5. When you are completely and fully relaxed, look at your list of solutions, then out loud say: "5-4-3-2-1 DECIDE!"
6. As you are saying that, your intuition will tell you which is the right solution.
7. Circle the right solution.
8. OR - if none of your solutions is the right one, your intuition will tell the right solution - write that down.
9. Next, write a short implementation plan for the right solution and DO IT - ACT ON IT immediately!
10. Stress relieved and problem solved.

Here is why this process works:
- Stress is usually caused by a part of you (ego-self) believing you do not have a choice in a situation. Yes, it's that simple.
- This creates a continuous tape-loop of anxiety thoughts running crazy in the back of your head.

- This means that you are focused on what you don't want and are creating more of it.
- When you write down a problem statement, you have stopped the tape-loop and moved those thoughts out of your head onto the paper in front of you where you can objectively see them for what they are.
- When you write down as many possible solutions you can think of - your ego-self now sees that there ARE solutions and that releases the stress. Also, you have now shifted your focus from the problem to the solutions - super important because you have now stopped creating more of the problem.
- When you relax into a meditative state, you can hear/feel/sense your intuition - the ultimate guide.
- When you say out loud: "5-4-3-2-1 DECIDE!", you are ensuring an intuitively-based decision and preventing your intellect and emotions from getting in the way. They take about 5 seconds to kick in. (Based on the excellent work of Mel Robbins).
- When you write a short implementation plan, you are totally focused on the solution and no longer the problem and that means you are now creating what you DO want. (Notice that you now feel good again).
- When you ACT ON IT immediately, you ensure success!
- All super-successful people run their lives via intuition and they ACT on it ASAP!

This process takes only a few minutes for each problem. Do you want to relieve all of your stress and solve all of your problems? Then write a list of all the problems running crazy in the back of your mind and do this process for each one!

**Ensure that you have fully and completely grieved all your losses and failures.

**Then CHOOSE to be happy, feel good and create your life as you wish. :)

Bonus 2: Goal Setting Worksheet

PLEASE READ THIS VERY CAREFULLY - THE SMALL DETAILS MATTER!

A research study was performed on Yale University graduates over a 30-year period. It was found that 3% of the grads were far happier, more fulfilled and more financially successful than the other 97% COMBINED! Think about that for a moment. Would you like to know what that 3% did differently? They had clear, written goals for every area of their lives!

Here's how to write effective goals...
Format: Please see the "GOALS TEMPLATE" below..
- Mission Statement - we each need a written mission statement at the top of the goals sheet. It is a declaration of who we are and what our place in the world is. Most companies have mission statements - we each need one also. Think about how you wish to be remembered.
- Determine all categories goals (i.e. financial/ career / charity, personal development/ educational/ spiritual, relationships/ family, housing/ transportation, leisure/ free time/ vacation, etc).

If you fail to write goals for any area of life - someone else will! What do you suppose your employer's goals are for you? To work more, harder and longer for less money! What do you suppose your family & friends' goals are for your time and money? They want it! What do you suppose advertisers' goals are for your time and money? They want it!

- Starting with the 1st area, write a concise goal (A COMPLETE SENTENCE) that meets the following SMART + AS-IF criteria:

1. Goals must be written as a complete sentence.
2. Each goal MUST be written AS-IF already achieved! Never say "I want" or "I will" or such future-tense words. Instead say: "I LOVE my ...." or "I LOVE that ...." or "I'm so happy now that…" or "I'm so grateful now that…"
3. Specific: The more specific the better. i.e. "I love my new car" is NOT specific. "I love my shiny brand new red electric Tesla Roadster convertible with tan leather interior that is easily affordable" IS specific. If your goal is to be married, you'd better have > 200 criteria for your spouse! Specific ensures that you can clearly and exactly visualize it.
4. Measurable: Your goals must be measurable. "I love being rich" is not measurable (or specific). "I love having passive income of >$25,000/month net, with annual increases of 20%" IS measurable.
5. Attainable & Realistic: When you write your goal, take special note of how you feel about it. Your subconscious will let you know whether you're full of it or not. If you've never earned more than $100,000/yr, then creating a goal of having an income > $250,000/month is not something your subconscious can accept - yet. Work up to it. Stretch your comfort zone but do it gradually. Only YOU know what's realistic for you right now.
6. Timely: While many teach that all goals must have a due date, I disagree. Putting a time limit on a goal creates urgency and

that creates separation and the inherent belief that the goal is not yet here. That is contrary to manifestation that requires that you have the exact same feeling NOW, as you will when it shows up in 3D. Please remove the "Due Date" column.

- Remember: these are criteria - not a part of your goals chart. After you have written a goal, check it to ensure it meets these criteria. Rewrite each goal CAREFULLY to ensure it meets all the criteria!
- After each goal write it's: Benefits, Potential Obstacles, Action Steps. Do this for each goal.
- Do this for each area of life for which you wish to be massively successful.
- Complete the page with the Insurance Statement: "All this or something better for the highest good of me and all concerned." Or write your own.
- Post on your bathroom mirror.

Never discuss with anyone but your spouse or people whom you are CERTAIN support you 100%. Not many people are capable of that. Modify and revise as needed – always right after the NEW MOON! Timing is everything!

When a goal is achieved, CELEBRATE IT!

Note: if you have difficulty deciding what you want, get another sheet of paper and write what you don't want. Then what you want will be clear.

Keep in mind the 80/20 rule. 20% of your activities produce 80% of your results. The other 80% of your time and energy does NOT further your goals. Often, the 20% is organizing, preparing (all mental) and getting started! This is true throughout the business world. Write out your primary goal and the action steps necessary to achieve it.

- Make sure you do something EVERY DAY that furthers your goal attainment!   Visualize with pure belief!
- If you haven't done something today that gets you closer to your goals, then the day did not get you closer to your goal!
- Choose every day to work on your primary goals! "Inspiration is pulling the chair up to the writing desk".

The universe rewards *inspired* ACTION!

Goals & Intentions

Mission Statement: I am a happy, healthy, successful, productive, motivated, intelligent, accomplished, joyful, loving, fun, balanced, satisfied person!
I utilize my talents in a way that is fun, fulfilling, massively profitable and provides service!

Goals	Benefits	Potential Obstacles	Action Steps	Due Date
Spiritual / Educational / Self-Improvement / Charity				
1				
2				
3				
Financial / Business /Career				
1				
2				
3				
Relationships		I AM a happy+healthy MULTIN		
1				
2		now!		
3				
Health				
1				
2				
3				
Recreation / Leisure				
1				
2				
3				
Home / Transportation				
1				
2				
3				

All this or something better right now for the highest good of me and all concerned! © MarcusGeier.com

Criteria: Specific, Measurable, Attainable, Realistic, Timely (due date), written AS-IF?

Bonus 3: Mirror Self-Talk Daily Ritual

All high-performing and super-successful people have a morning ritual to get them into peak state. That is the single most vital part of their day.

Here is a proven and powerful daily ritual/process that will do 2 things for you.

> You will start each day on a "high", self-empowered, enthusiastic, vital and "on-fire"!
> - This will cause those around you to respond in ever more positive ways, or fall away.
> - You will attack each day with enhanced vitality, clarity and peace - thus accomplish much more by doing less - and with an ever-deepening joy.
>
> In a matter of days, this will begin reprogramming your sabotaging subconscious beliefs.
> - This will transform your entire life experience with ever more automagical synchronicities!
> - You will find that you still have "ups" and "downs", but soon your "downs" will be higher than your previous "ups"! That is a most exciting realization!

1. Every morning, 1st thing, go look in mirror into your eyes.
2. Smile lovingly! (like you mean it)
3. Point, open-handed at your image.
4. Say (out loud), an affirmation like: "You know [YourName], you're a really wonderful person!"
5. Point, open-handed back at yourself and gently tap upper chest bone (thymus gland).
6. While tapping, say (out loud), a reflection like: "Yes I am!"
7. Repeat with varying affirmations.

8. Do for 2-10 minutes until feeling AWESOME! Don't stop until you do! Some mornings it'll take 2 minutes, other mornings it'll take 10 minutes. Do NOT stop until you are in peak state!

9. Ensure affirmations are things your subconscious can accept. I.e: can't say "you're a 3 meter tall, flaming-haired, multi-billionaire" - subconscious won't believe and will be counter-productive. Can say: "I am attracting more and more money every day!" Or: "Every day in every way _____ is getting better and better!" You can write them out ahead of time if you wish. Note: spend some quality time in a meditative state with a notebook and ask your subconscious to tell you your sabotaging beliefs. Write affirmations to counter them. Good ones are: "You, _____ deserve____"

10. If you commit to doing this every morning (at least) for 30 days, your life will be transformed!

11. This is a well proven, powerful reprogramming technique. It works wonderfully!

12. To super-charge it, do the following

13. Every evening spend 2 minutes with your journal reviewing your day and identifying the wonderful little synchronicities, unexpected surprises/gifts that happened that day. Write them down. Start looking for them next day and you will find more and more automagically! Your days will become treasure-hunts filled with eager expectation to see what wonderful gifts the universe will provide to you that day. They will increase.

14. After 30 days, spend ½ hour with your journal reflecting on how changed you are since 30 days prior.

15. Feel Gratitude! "Thank You! Thank You! Thank You!" Let that become your continual mantra.

16. Keep doing this! Do more of what works and less of what does not work.

17. Watch your life get better and better!

What do you expect will happen when you commit to doing this every day for 30 days?

- You will start each day on an energy high, eager, expectant and joyful.
- The people around you will react far more positively and your relationships, both personal and business will be hugely enhanced.
- This will result in significantly greater happiness, health and success.
- What will it cost you? About 5-10 minutes in the morning.
- Will you do it?

Bonus 4: A quick reprogramming tool - with example.

This is a process of using your imagination to rewrite the script of a traumatic experience into a version that you want. Your brain literally does not know the difference between a "real" experience and a vividly imagined one! Your "real" experience only exists as a memory in your brain. It has no other reality. Your "vividly imagined" experience only exists as a memory in your brain. It has no other reality. They are the same. You can consciously choose to replace one with the other. It is really that simple. You can rewrite your past the way you would have wanted it to be, trauma by trauma. If we are the product of our past (all of our experiences), then choosing to rewrite past traumas and replace old memories will literally create a new you!

So, how can you identify your sabotaging beliefs?
- Consider the recurrent undesirable patterns in your life and ask: "What would I have to unconsciously believe to keep recreating this sort of experience?"
- Enlist the help of a close friend or partner to monitor your speech. The words and wording we use when we're not paying attention reveal our beliefs. Ask them to help you identify your beliefs.

Here's one way to reprogram:
- Go someplace very quiet and relax into a meditative space with eyes closed.

- Take the time to really go deep via deep, slow breathing.
- Consider a core sabotaging belief.
  - I.e. I am powerless.
- Remember a childhood experience that caused (or reinforced) that belief.
  - *I.e: Chris (my older brother) would frequently try out his new wrestling moves and pin me to the floor. I was completely helpless and he wouldn't get off. This was massively traumatic to my young self. My worst fear is being put in a strait jacket or getting stuck in a narrow tunnel.*
  - *My parents yelled and argued extremely loudly a lot and I felt vulnerable and powerless.*
  - *My other brother and sister often took out their helplessness on me via beating, teasing and yelling.*
- Re-imagine that experience as you wish it were.
  - *Using my imaginary super-powers, I simply turn off gravity for a while so that Chris and I float in the air. Then I hug him and tell him I love him. He can't help but release me with love and a smile!*
  - *When Dad & Mom are yelling - I simply walk up to them, bring and hold their hands together and tell them I love them. They are helpless to resist.*
  - *I wander through the house and whenever my sister or brother approach me I say: "I Love You!" They then approach with love.*
- I AM EMPOWERED - ALWAYS!!

Remember, all super-successful people rigorously do their daily am rituals to keep themselves in peak state. **<u>That is essential!</u>**

> The daily mirror self talk ritual above is great,
> Also EFT (see Brad Yates on Youtube),
> Watch/listen daily to inspirational/motivational talks on Youtube and elsewhere.
> Put on energizing music and dance wildly around your house yelling affirmations.
> Do whatever it takes to keep returning to the empowered, excited, optimistic and joyous state!

This doesn't happen TO you - it happens FROM you.

Note: As you rise, those who aren't congruent will fall away and be replaced by those who are. That's ok, let them go.

Note: When you can honestly get to the place where feeling really awesome is the only important experience for you (joy, happiness, vitality, satisfaction), and the goals no longer matter (house, car, money, mate, health resolution), then you will see magic in your life.

You are magnificently blessed - if you choose to see it.
I'm standing by to help you!

PLEASE:

Leave a kind review

for this book

but please

do NOT disclose the formula

in your review!

Thank you!

Bonus 5: Amazing Opportunity For You Right Now!

Do you REALLY want to make the **FASTEST** possible progress toward your dream life?

Then go to www.marcusgeier.com right now and sign up for 6 months of personal mentoring/coaching! It's completely affordable and will produce huge ROI.

Accountability and twice-monthly regular coaching is by far, the best way to make massive progress.

If you have a business, or know business owners with 15+ employees, I'd love the opportunity to speak with them/you about how I can increase their employees' productivity by 20%+ and increase retention and job satisfaction.

I'm happily available for rousing keynote speaking, seminars, classes and group training in mindset, business strategy, marketing & branding strategy, negotiation and metaphysics.

Marcus Geier Bio

Marcus is Earth's first fully certified Metaphysical Philanthropist. He is a highly accomplished metaphysician, having studied/practised intensely for over 57 years, including a formal apprenticeship of 20 years, from age 3.

He has had long careers in real estate investments, business valuation and investment, and equities day-trading. He was an award-winning business professor for 13 years (always among the top 1% faculty in student surveys).

Next, Marcus worked with a large, premier international wealth and success coaching organization as the head in-house coach, strategic business analyst and coach's coach. He has successfully coached over 3,300 (so far) clients in 47 countries with a 98.7% "WOW" rate. His uncanny ability to root out a client's underlying blocks, and help them reprogram on the spot, has produced a depth of raving testimonials that make him blush.

Combining a deeply powerful intuitive ability with extensive business experience and knowledge, he melds the two into an unparalleled client experience of multidimensional transformation. Marcus has sifted through a massive number of systems, teachings, processes and belief complexes to arrive at an efficient understanding of how life works.

As a clairsentient & clairsavant empath, Marcus has been facilitating self-transformation seminars with his wife, "MoonCoach"™ Silvia Pancaro for many years.

Marcus has authored 3 books to date:
1. ***"Blueprint of Happiness"***,
2. ***"The Ultimate Success Formula"***
3. ***"The Life-Coaching Bible"***

Marcus is a consummate pain-remover.

www.marcusgeier.com
www.right.coach
www.metaphysicalphilanthropist.com
www.successtiming.com

www.ingramcontent.com/pod-product-compliance
Lightning Source LLC
Chambersburg PA
CBHW072225170526
45158CB00002BA/762